Girl Chasing

To my BEST FRIEND
CHRIS DAVIES

THIS HANDBOOK GOES

WITH THE

"MATTHEWS COURSE"

Rolf
1/MAY/95

Girl Chasing

HOW TO IMPROVE YOUR GAME

CATHY HOPKINS
Cartoons by Gray Jolliffe

HarperCollins*Publishers*

HarperCollins*Publishers*
77–85 Fulham Palace Road,
Hammersmith, London W6 8JB

This paperback edition 1994
1 3 5 7 9 8 6 4 2

Previously published in paperback by Fontana 1992
Reprinted once

First published in Great Britain by
Angus & Robertson (UK) 1989
Reprinted twice

ISBN 0 00 637940 0

Set in Garamond

Printed in Great Britain by
Scotprint Ltd, Musselburgh

CONTENTS

INTRODUCTION

Girl Chasing has been a favourite sport among men for many years now. It is played in every country in the world (even Russia) and is without doubt the one game that cuts across national barriers and links all men with a common understanding.

It is the one totally universal sport. After all, they play hardly any cricket in Mongolia and do very little swimming in Spitzbergen, but even in the remotest outposts of the world, Girl Chasing has become increasingly popular. In fact, its adherents increase in direct proportion to the population, which is an interesting point for sociologists and statisticians to ponder. Even some women are starting to take it up...but this book doesn't cover the intricacies of *that* branch of the sport.

Quite recently, in order to make the game more difficult and therefore more interesting the rules have been changed slightly. The apron-clad creature at the sink burnt her bra and Mr Macho was suddenly jerk of the month. Girls (throughout the book 'Girls' in the context of 'Girl Chasing' means any female from sixteen to 106) discovered who they were. They discovered what they didn't want. Men still know what they want but are no longer any too sure of what they're up against. But life goes on. Girls are still being chased. And getting caught.

After many years of research, mostly empirical, involving myself and a wide spectrum of female acquaintances I have reached the seminal conclusions contained in this book. My aim is not to assist the men who already play the game expertly, but to widen our field of choice by getting more of you chaps into play – and *au fait* with the new rules.

1

FIRST IMPRESSIONS

> *'Her dress was so damned tight*
> *I could hardly breathe'*
> * – Benny Hill*

As far as encounters with women go, many men feel totally out of their depth. They find it a mysterious game where the rules change dramatically with each new player.

With no hard and fast rules, with more strategies and permutations of play than mahjong, and with nothing, up to now, written down, anyone seriously considering Girl Chasing needs to be well prepared, dedicated and preferably (though not necessarily) rich.

You've got to be smart too. Modern girls do not take kindly to slobs and dummies. We are tough cookies but well worth a little effort.

So let's start on the task of perfecting your appeal and polishing your presentation.

One thing that should be abundantly clear is that while girls appreciate a good-looking bloke, looks are rarely the main attraction. If they were, hardly any of you would ever get laid.

How many times, for example, have you thought, 'What on earth does she see in him?' The answer of course is that he is probably a 'pro' Girl Chaser.

Men, and I'm generalizing here, tend to look at a girl and either think 'Yes Please', or 'No thanks', often without even realizing it on a conscious level. Snap decisions. 'I like mine but I don't think much of yours.' You know the type of thing. Dogs sniff each other's bottoms in much the same way.

Girls however are more subtle. Here are some factors that can explain the apparent inconsistencies in what women find attractive in men. Factors which rarely impinge on a man's desire for a woman.

CHEMISTRY

Usually apparent to both parties. It lacks time, blurs vision, turns your head to helium, legs to jelly, heart to cream caramel and freezes you to the spot. Girls often go blotchy round the collarbone area, which is a dead giveaway. Men tend to turn into gibbering idiots and get their lines back to front. A sensitive woman recognizes this for what it is and is flattered rather than put off by it. Over-confidence can be a turn-off in civilized societies like ours, while it goes down a treat in South Africa.

AGE

Some girls like old men and some girls like young men. Me, I've got one of each but I'm just greedy. So if you're a tubby tum, greying at the temples and fraying at the edges, don't despair. There's always a market for 'toy' dirty old men.

FREUDIAN SLIP. FORGIVABLE AS LONG AS IT ISN'T PART OF A DELIBERATE STRATEGY.

PHASES

You may consider yourself to be a heart-throb, but fail miserably with your intended victim because she's into the 'pale, tortured artist' image this year. Many girls are only attracted to what's 'in' for them at any particular phase in their lives.

Examples of these are: Political men; Religious men; Decadent men (very popular); Materialistic men; Sporty men; Rough, nasty and horrid men (a big favourite).

So one of the first things the Girl Chaser must do is try to suss out what phase or type she's into. Then if at all possible he should adapt, chameleon-like, to that role. If you're a sporty type and find it difficult to change into an intellectual, though, don't waste your time. Find yourself another girl to chase. It's not worth doing your brains in trying to pass yourself off as something you're not.

BACKGROUND

She could be riddled with class consciousness or even religion. If so, she's looking for someone who's acceptable to Mummy and Daddy.

But again, never pretend. Be what you are and settle for a one-night stand. If you pretend to be Jewish, for instance, the moment you get lucky could be the moment you get caught out.

CONDITIONING

When you see her for the first time and go 'Cor!' and start drooling and acting like an idiot, you'll have no idea what's been going on in her life up till then. So don't go assuming she's a bad girl just out of wishful thinking. She may be one of the trendy new celibates, which is a tricky one to crack, what with all the anti-sex propaganda flying around these days.

So ask her lots of questions, but not so many that she thinks you're plain nosey rather than interested. Try to find out things like:

— Has she had a bad time with a man and needs to be needed?
— Is she having a great time with men and needs to be independent?
— Are you a pussy cat and she's looking for a tiger?
— Are you a macho man, and she's looking for a wimp to kick around?

Once you've found out a few things about her it's time to start trotting out some of your strong points. Here are a few things that impress girls about men. If you don't have all of them try

to have at least one. And if you can't even manage one, forget
Girl Chasing and take up darts:

> *A sense of humour. Intelligence. Generosity.*
> *Good manners. A big willie (it's the size, not*
> *what you do with it.) Good looks. Money.*
> *Power. A nice bum. Style. A vulnerable little-*
> *boy-lost act. A genuine liking for women.*
> *Clean fingernails. And last, but by no means*
> *least, a genetic ability to lick your eyebrows.*

2

HOW TO MEET WOMEN

> *'Don't blame your circumstances, change them. To get on in the world get up and look for the circumstances you want and if you can't find them, make them'*
> *– George Bernard Shaw (sort of)*

Approximately 50 per cent of the people in the world are women. So any man who says he never meets any, either has to be blind, a recluse, or in jail. If he's not any of these things he doesn't deserve to meet any.

The best places to get to know girls are places where there's no urgency to score, places where you won't need witty chat-up lines. This includes the office, your college or, if you're really desperate, a local embroidery class. The main thing is to have a serious shared interest, then one thing automatically leads to another. Some women love horse-riding and keep-fit classes, so try getting into that. Also, turn everyday events into opportunities to meet women. Girls in supermarkets and working at petrol stations are far more approachable than when they're tarted up at the local disco, wary of being picked up unless it's by George Michael.

Of course, if you have lots of confidence, good looks, and some good chat-up lines and are not too worried about

Mathematicians reckon the odds against this cliché are 582933 billion to one, so don't count on it.

competition from other predatory males there's nothing too wrong with parties, wine bars, clubs and discos. However, discos are out if you rely more on chat than looks, simply because of the noise factor. There's nothing less romantic than screaming something into a bimbo's ear and her shouting 'What?' Also, bear in mind that our disco sisters are rarely brain surgeons, so save the more subtle of your chat lines for more discerning ears, and a quieter ambience.

Good places for shy men to meet girls

At work
At college
In a wine bar with friends

In a convent
In hospital with a broken leg (not recommended)
At a gym
Through small ads in *Time Out* or *Private Eye*
At a dinner party
Pottery classes

Other good ways to meet girls

In the lingerie department of a department store
At the perfume counter
In the street
Dancing
On a singles holiday

Getting their phone number from a friend and phoning them
   out of the blue
In the launderette

In bed (unusual, but possible)
At the VD clinic
Hang around with your sister

The last one can be very useful if you have a co-operative sister
or female cousin as all girls know at least ten others, and it is
far easier for them to strike up a conversation with an attractive
girl merely by asking where she got the lovely sweater. Then
it's only natural for you to join in, and the ice having been
broken it's up to you to sink or swim.

The main thing is to have an enthusiastic rather than a defeatist attitude. Enthusiasm can win us over just as easily as good looks or money (well nearly as easily).

3

WHAT KIND OF GIRL ARE YOU CHASING?

> *'There are two types of women;*
> *Goddesses and doormats'*
> *– Picasso*

Well of course Picasso was well known for his attitude to women, so statements like that are only to be expected.

a)   DOORMAT   b) GODDESS

But to an extent he's got a point, except there's a bit of both in most of us and the part that shows most can depend on the man we're with.

We all know talented pretty girls who limp silently along in the shadow of some attractive brute, wanting nothing more than his approval. Usually he ends up showing her the door and welcomes in the next contestant.

If that's the sort of player you want to be you'll end up frustrated and unhappy, because as you get older you'll find talented pretty doormats increasingly difficult to find. Nobody loves a wrinkly bully boy.

Girls, however, can appear such a mysterious and multi-faceted species. Who'd have thought that the sweetheart on Reception would turn out to be a nagging harridan after only three dates, or that the capable, gorgeous lady who ought to have it all lets men walk over her one after the other.

Most of you men know exactly what you want in an ideal world. It's the Goddess. She's an unmistakable ten with a body to die for and she knows it. She's funny and flirty and dresses to kill, and most of us less fortunate girls hate her to bits.

Eve was one of these, and don't believe those old Biblical paintings. She was the original good-time girl identifiable only in that she never wore any knickers, a fact which was not missed by Adam. Some people say it was the apple that tempted him, but we all know better. . . . Since then even the most serious and rational of you are prone to having your brains scrambled by the very thought of a girl with a bare bottom under her frock.

Of course since Eve's day a lot of sub-species have sprung up to confuse and bewilder you. The following chart, 'The Evolution of Eve', is intended to help you identify why the female psyche is so complicated and to remind you that behind any one smiling persona lurk the genes of hundreds of others . . . Identifying your victim is a big clue to Girl Chasing, with this chart you can understand the girl you're chasing and others you may have chased in the past.

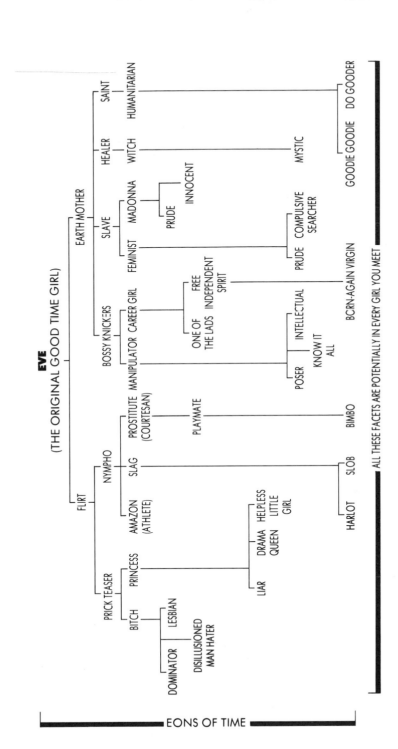

4

THE OPENING GAMBIT

> 'Compliment every woman you meet;
> If you get 5 per cent on your outlay
> it's a good investment'
> – Arnold Bennett

It's difficult though, isn't it? The fear of rejection is the hardest thing to overcome. Many a fragile Girl Chaser's ego has been deeply wounded by a sneering response to his plucky attempt to get talking.

He: Want to come back to my place to play hunt the banana?

She: Usually I never forget a face. In your case I'll make an exception [Exit. Disdainfully]

The answer is practice. Not in front of a mirror, but in the field, out there where the girls are. Once you've been rejected enough times you'll become immune; after that it will be water off a drake's back. And on the plus side, by the law of averages alone, you're bound to get lucky now and again.

This old gag is an extreme example of what I mean:

Fred: How do you meet pretty girls?

Jim: I just walk over to them and say 'How about a bonk'?

Fred: You must get an awful lot of slaps in the face.
Jim: Yeah, but I get an awful lot of bonks as well!

PERSEVERANCE AND THE HIDE OF
AN ELEPHANT CAN BRING RESULTS

Needless to say the crude approach is not a good idea unless you're operating in the red light district, or happen to be a famous rock star. To most girls, being disgusting is sudden death and you'll blow your chances of what might otherwise have been an interested (or interesting) party.

If you're doing your chasing out of doors you might benefit by some of these useful props:

a) A dog — the cuter the better. Try a Spaniel or an Old English Sheepdog. Girls will fall over themselves to ask if they can stroke it (to which, of course, you may reply, 'Certainly, and you can stroke the dog too if you want').

DOG USAGE:

Hi Gorgeous!

a) Ventriloquism

b) Dog as ice-breaker

b) A camera. Ask her to take a picture of you so you can send it to your mother. Then you can take a picture of her for your new exhibition of pretty faces.

c) A streetplan. Wander around aimlessly and ask her for directions. If she tells you to get lost you can say you already are.

Women like men with a sense of humour, so a funny opening line isn't a bad idea. But don't forget that, while a chat-up line can be well rehearsed, anything can happen in the next sentence, so you'll have to ad lib and that's where you can come unstuck.

Example :

    He: 'Hi — you look as if you know something the rest of us don't!'

> She: 'I do. I'm a bloke'
> He: 'Er . . . um . . .'

Of course it helps if you think a girl fancies you. We girls have subtle ways of showing this which may be difficult to recognize.

Tell-tale things women do if they see a chap they like the look of:

    a) Ignore him
    b) Flirt with his mate
    c) Go scarlet
    d) Go home
    e) Stick their tongue in his ear

The last of these, though unusual, requires little or no follow-on chat from the male. It also implies an advanced state of inebriation, so if you're lucky enough for it to happen to you don't just stand there, go for it.

Luckily, women see more attractive things in the most ordinary of men than you'd ever believe possible. So if you're not particularly good looking don't fret — Someone, Somewhere, is waiting up for you, with your big ears and pointed head. Amazing isn't it?

A tip to find out if she's interested is to:

    a) Make eye contact
    b) Move out of her eyeline
    c) Hide behind a pillar (or a pillock)
    d) Watch to see if her eyes look to where she last saw you and then search the room
    e) If they do, you've got it made
    f) Wait a minute then wander over

Do *not* say:
    'Drop 'em blossom, you're on next'!

Do say:

'God has sent me to you. He says you have a nice ass'
Other possible opening lines are:

'I'm glad you don't recognise me — I want people to like me for myself, not my money'

'You look like a virgin. Fortunately I specialise in such diseases'

'You're a beautiful woman, but your eyes tell me you lead a sheltered life'

'I can't dance, but I'd love to hold you while you do'

'And you — what do *you* dream about?'

'Hi, I'm Joe, and I'd be happy to listen to all your problems'

'Can I borrow your glue?'

'Knock, knock . . .'

'I'm madly in love with you, I'd die for you, I can't live without you, please, please be mine forever!'

She: 'Sorry I don't want to get into anything serious'

You: 'Who's being serious?'

Other things to bear in mind about your prospective 'chasee'.

Most women love rebels.

Most women are pushovers for flattery, particularly the beautiful ones who never get enough because everyone assumes they get too much.

Most women can spot bullshit a mile away.

FIND A WAY TO MAKE
HER SPEAK FIRST :

Most women know their weak points and are extremely aware of their attributes, so look for these and remark on them. If you notice what's special about her she'll know you're on the level, and pretty astute as well.

> 'The best way to turn a woman's head
> is to tell her she has a beautiful profile'
> – Sacha Guitry

Most women love making history. By this I mean if the moment you start to chat her up the waiter happens to spill a tray of drinks over you it will be something she can talk about for years. "The moment I met Brian he got two Pina Coladas down his shirt front." She'll be all yours after that. And waiters can be bribed.

Lastly, don't feel obliged to be witty in your initial approach. The Mr Nice Guy, perfect gentleman technique is gaining ground these days and a bit of simple old-fashioned charm and honesty rarely goes amiss.

5

FLIRTING AND THE FOLLOW-THROUGH

> 'Women have a lot of faults
> Men have only two,
> Everything they say,
> and everything they do'
> – Leonara Strumpfenburg

We girls know you're a klutz. All men have this disadvantage from the word go, and we get a perverse pleasure out of watching you trying to bluff your way through. It's also what makes us love you.

So after you wander over and stun us with your magical opening ice-breaker we are either screaming with laughter or screaming with laughter on the inside and waiting for what comes next. Which is usually small talk – let's face it, we're not all comediennes.

The thing is that we know pretty well straight away whether we could possibly end up in bed with you. If it's unthinkable, all the chat in the world isn't going to make a blind bit of difference. On the other hand, if we fancy you and sigh an inner 'Yes Please' we're not about to let you know just yet. But there are signs for you to look for, little clues we give out that might give you a hint of our incipient co-operation. The snag is, of course, that men are about as subtle as an air raid and rarely spot these signs of arousal short of her pulling her dress up over her head.

> 'She may be English, but the look in her eyes is international'

Try looking at her eyes. If she keeps eye contact she could be interested. If she looks away she could still be interested. You never know.

Try studying her body language. Does she lean towards you? If you're sitting do her knees point in your direction?

Does she mirror your every posture?

Is she relaxed if you touch her briefly? Or does she stiffen and fold her arms?

Psychologists tell us all these things mean something, but maybe they don't. That's women for you.

Anyway, pretty soon you'll start to get the picture, unless you're a total dodo. What if she doesn't seem to be at all interested? It doesn't necessarily mean you should give it up and move on. Women love to be persuaded, to be won over, to be seduced. It's part of the game.

Even so, it's also important not to come on too strong at first unless the response is obviously there. Men who stand too close when you've just met them are a pain.

Flirting is fun. True flirts can't help themselves – they do it with all women, even grannies and mothers-in-law. There's a lot to be said for being a flirt. Women are wonderful if you're wonderful to them, and the more you practise the better you get – it builds your confidence, so that when you find someone you really like you don't drool like a blithering idiot or dry up.

It's an old cliché, but you get back what you give out. So if you want the goodies, be generous in spirit.

BODY LANGUAGE – POINTS TO CONSIDER:

1) Is this girl....

   a) Showing interest by reflecting his pose?

   b) Taking the piss?

2) Is this girl....

   a) Pointing her knees in his direction to show she fancies him?

   b) Paralytic drunk?

TIPS FOR FLIRTING

Practise different looks for showing interest (wide-eyed, prolonged eye contact, fleeting but meaningful glance). Make her laugh. Flatter her. Be cheeky but not pushy. Be bright-eyed and enthusiastic. Accidentally brush her hand. And above all keep it light. And when it's all going well and you've got her interest, leave. There's always another time, and she'll want to see you again, particularly as you didn't try anything physical this time.

Some don'ts of flirting

Don't get serious
Don't wait for her to make the first move
Don't get clingy
Don't do it to make someone else jealous
Don't only flirt with women you fancy – you'll get rusty
Don't do it when you're drunk, tired, depressed or suffering from severe acne and greasy hair.

How To SPOT AN INCURABLE FLIRT:

6

REJECTION

> *'The more beautiful they are the more eager they are for me to hit on them so they can say no'*
> *– Al Goldstein*

Rejection is what happens in the early stages, so it's not to be confused with more complicated things like separation or divorce.

But it's still a pain, so you have to be prepared for it to happen, because if you're a Girl Chaser it's going to happen quite a lot.

The consoling thing is the more it happens the less you worry about it. That's why rejection is always tougher on handsome men.

But guard against being a habitual rejectee, or you could develop the 'Groucho Syndrome'. This means that when you do eventually find someone who likes you, you'll probably think something must be the matter with her, and not follow through.

Don't take rejection personally — it could be explained in any of the following ways:

1) She could be married (check for rings or handcuff abrasions)
2) She could be spoken for (even worse)

3) She's had a long, hard day
4) She's been burgled; had a car crash; etc
5) She's only interested in rich rock stars
6) She's only interested in women (why not, so are you)
7) She's celibate
8) She's a man in drag
9) She's a spoilt bad-mannered brat
10) You're an incredible jerk

The last one of these brings us to other ways you can get rejected in which you only have yourself to blame:

1) Talk non-stop
2) Brag about your Porsche
3) Ask the same question twice

4) Act desperate (women hate tripping over a man's tongue)
5) Get drunk because you're nervous
6) Look around the room at other girls when she's talking
7) Brag about your ex-girlfriends
8) Be too available
9) Wear dirty clothes
10) Have green suede teeth, dirty fingernails, greasy hair, BO, bad breath and dandruff

Easy isn't it?

7

ABOUT YOUR TECHNIQUE

> 'Candy is Dandy,
> But liquor is quicker'
> – Ogden Nash

THE NO-TECHNIQUE TECHNIQUE
(For The Smart Girl)

The best technique agreed by experienced Girl Chasers throughout the world is the No-Technique Technique.

Of course this is the most difficult technique there is because it requires intelligence, maturity and a genuine high regard for women in general. You must also be a good loser, able to shrug off your failures with a philosophical smile. Basically it helps to be over forty.

Because the No-Technique Technique has, as the name implies, no technique, it is difficult to give any instructions or even pointers as to how it is supposed to work. However, these guidelines may be of some value:

1) Treat every woman as the unique individual she is
2) Let your response to her be entirely natural and in keeping with the moment, the mood and the place you're in

3) Try listening to what she says in answer to your questions
4) Use pauses and silences rather than try to cover them up
5) Forget stereotyped images of girls and how you're 'supposed' to treat us
6) Forget what worked with the last one

THE 'NO TECHNIQUE' TECHNIQUE IN ACTION

THE CREEPING UP ON HER TECHNIQUE
(For The Hard to Get)

Believe it or not familiarity can often breed lust. If she sees you around often enough and you don't seem to be attached you can grow on a girl.

1) You meet her at a party
2) You give her a bit of prolonged eye contact — enough to say 'I'm interested' then ignore her
3) Find out from mutual friends where she spends her free time, and start hanging out there. Make more eyes at her — but *do not* stare, because that looks desperate and goofy
4) Next time ignore her again. This should start to make her intrigued
5) Make verbal contact but keep it brief
6) Strike cool poses and wear trendy clothes
7) By now she should be picking up the signals and it's time to ask her out on a date

By the end of all this she will either be mad about you or think you are a total and utter wanker. But it's worth a try if you can't think of anything else.

THE I'VE GOT A PORSCHE TECHNIQUE
(For Bimbos)

This only works with bimbos, or incredibly stupid girls with white shoes from Essex. It helps to have white shoes yourself.

1) First find a bimbo, because it isn't going to cut any ice with anyone else

2) Walk over with a huge bunch of keys dangling from your belt. Another good prop is a lambswool sweater with the arms tied round your waist from behind — oh, and sunglasses on the top of your head
3) Say 'Hi, I've got a Porsche'
4) Drive off with her at great speed before someone comes along with a Ferrari

FAST CAR PERSON MISTAKENLY
TRYING TO PULL GIRL WITH 'A' LEVELS

Of course, and you may have spotted this, the Porsche Technique does require you to have a Porsche, and that's the catch. It doesn't have to be a 911 — it can be a 'pretend' Porsche like a 928 or 924. . . .

THE NEW AGE MAN TECHNIQUE
(For New Age Girls)

1) Wear a Fair-Isle jumper and open-toed sandals
2) Carry a good selection of books on self-development — *The Man/Woman Relationship, The Cinderella Complex* should do it
3) Compliment her on her natural look — hairy legs, unshaved armpits
4) Tell her you're really getting in touch with your feelings and your female side
5) Cook her a healthy meal and give her an aromatic massage afterwards
6) Be prepared to be abandoned for the next charismatic macho boy who happens along

Many girls say they want a 'nice' man who'll accept them and they can talk to but tend to kick sand in his face when they find him.

THE SMILING NAZI TECHNIQUE
(For Masochistic Girls)

1) Keep her guessing. Treat her like you've found a soulmate all night then don't call her for weeks.
2) Keep her unsettled, eager to please. Talk to her like

a princess, then treat her like a slave.

3) Confuse her into submission — cheap meal in a naff venue (and get her to pay) then blindfold her and serve her "cristal" on ice and spoonfeed her beluga caviar when you get home.

The police use this one. It's called the bad guy, nice guy technique. It works. It worked in the film *9½ Weeks*.

THE EVER SO MODEST TECHNIQUE
(For The Girl Who's Seen And Heard it All)

This is the flip-side of the Porsche approach. Firstly, you really do have to have some good things going for you, like a lot of dosh, or brains, or a big willie, and the girl you're chasing has to be intelligent. What you do *not* do is refer directly to your goodies, but leak them gradually and only if she asks. She'll be greatly impressed by your reticence.

> *All women like men with money, but not if they're flash with it. A French cynic once wrote: "Women never marry a man for his money – they fall in love with him first".*

1) Never talk about your car. She'll notice it's an Aston Martin Convertible when she gets in it
2) Tell her you have a little place in the sticks. Sooner or later she'll find out it's a mansion
3) Tell her you're busy on Tuesday night, but not why. If she happens to switch on the TV and see you on a chat show all well and good — otherwise she'll probably hear about it from her friends

4) If she asks where you were educated say you went to college. If she presses you, admit it was Balliol, Oxford
5) Jokingly tell her you're no great shakes as a lover — she's bound to want to find out for herself

Even little things can impress a girl using this technique. Things that she finds out about you gradually will be all the more exciting — think of all the movies you have seen where the handsome prince wins the hand of the fair maiden by posing as a pauper.

The Ever So Modest Technique, for obvious reasons, is not for a one-night stand. But the trouble is she'll probably fall in love with you, which may not be what you want either.

THE ABSOLUTE ROTTER TECHNIQUE
(For The Naive Girl)

If you're a nasty person and relentless with it you can pull many girls by promising them anything.

1) 'I'm expecting a huge cheque in a couple of months. I'll take you shopping in Bond Street'
2) 'Let's go to Paris for dinner when we get to know each other a little better'
3) 'I'd love to be on holiday with you — somewhere nice and warm, maybe later in the year I'll arrange it'

Three rules to this technique: soft tone of voice (seductive, unaggressive); old-fashioned manners; undivided attention (you must behave as if thoroughly enchanted).

The idea is to lull her into a false sense of security. You seem so obviously to want to spend more than an evening with her that it can bring about a willingness to cooperate physically all the sooner. Which she probably will, and as you have no conscience you won't mind dumping her in the morning.

This is a rotter's approach but, if considered philosophically, is an education for most girls.

THE STRONG, MOODY, SILENT TECHNIQUE
(For Rich Older Women With Boring Husbands)

If you're good looking, but worried about the fact that you were last in the queue when they were dishing out brains, this one is probably your best bet.

Hang around looking:
     a) Strong   b) Moody   c) Silent

It isn't a bad idea to have a Georgio Armani suit to go with it. On no account open your mouth unless it's to accommodate a Gauloise. But be warned, this technique rarely works unless you really are a *hunk*, in which case she may drop 'em so fast she gets scorch marks on her knees.

THE HAIRDRESSER TECHNIQUE
(For All Types)

This one is good because you talk non-stop about her. Compliment her hair, ask her where she has it done. Talk to her about clothes, fashion and magazines. Ask her where she's going on holiday, and tell her you bet she looks great with a tan and a bikini.

To do all this well, it's a great help if you're gay, and she'll realize that. So you'll have to prove you're not and that could be fun. Women love the way gay men behave towards them, you often find them saying things like, 'Adrian would be the perfect man if only he was straight.' In fact, come to think of it, giving the impression you're as camp as a row of pink tents isn't a bad idea to start with. Women love to reform men. Which brings me on to the next technique:

THE BORN BAD-ASS TECHNIQUE
(For Girls With Cement For Brains)

Being a misfit or a criminal or simply anti-authority is fascinating for many girls. And if you're a drunk or a drug addict to boot so much the better. The fact is that you can benefit two ways from this. First you'll score with the born

reformers who'll see it as their mission in life to make you mend your ways, and secondly you'll be a big hit with the girl who can't resist a rebel. Look how many women hang out with terrorists, Hells Angels, Pimps and East End villains. The Patty Hearst Syndrome is alive and well and residing in the bosom of many an unlikely young lady. Find out if they were convent-educated and you'll be half way there.

THE GO-FOR-IT TECHNIQUE

Don't beat about the bush, tell her exactly what you want (as if she didn't already know). This approach is advised only if you're short of time because you have just been warned of an imminent nuclear attack and like the idea of going out with a bang. Other than that, quite frankly, it's a bit of a bummer.

THE LITTLE BOY TECHNIQUE
(For Maternal Girls)

The purpose of this one is to tap a woman's maternal instincts, so you have to want a mother substitute if you try it.

1) Dress in an endearingly dishevelled way (like you need help with your ironing, not your personal hygiene)
2) Act adventurous but doolally. Mischievous but charming.
3) When faced with anything domestic, look confused. If asked to help with the washing-up, drop plates everywhere. A useful line is, 'I boiled

an egg for half an hour once and the bloody
thing was still hard'
4) Make out you haven't eaten properly for weeks –
just chips and beans
5) Lard it on about how you've been hurt by
women in the past, and how lonely you are
because you're so wary of getting into another
close relationship

If this is done with the right combination of helplessness and
charm, she will have an intense desire to smother you in her
ample bosom and make you cry with happiness. But the
charm is important otherwise you'll simply be a wimp.

THE BUDDY TECHNIQUE
(For Girls at a Party)

This is where you hunt in pairs with a close friend and you
take it in turns to help each other at parties etc. It was
perfected by Murray Roman, the American comedian.

1) Your buddy sidles up to the girl you want and
says, 'Hey, you see that guy over there [pointing
at you], he's a real wolf. Don't let him anywhere
near you, you'll only get hurt'
2) She says, 'Thanks for the warning but I can take
care of myself'
3) You then move in and she's intrigued and
desperate to prove you can't pull her
4) When she discovers you're a pussy cat she jumps
on you out of relief. Well, maybe

Lastly, you can try:

THE NEW CELIBATE MALE TECHNIQUE
(For Girls Who Like a Challenge)

You: 'I really like you, but right now I'm practising celibacy'

Her: 'Oh that's silly . . .'

You: 'I'm sorry but I'm channelling all my sexual energy into my work'

Her: 'Come on — surely you can put a little of that energy into my channel?'

You: 'Well . . . OK then just this once, but it's only because I really like you . . .'

8

THE FIRST DATE

> *'I've had a really wonderful*
> *evening – but this wasn't it'*
> *– Groucho Marx*

The first date should always be somewhere out of the ordinary, which usually means expensive. And you'll be doing the paying because you did the asking.

On no account take her to the movies. First dates are about talking, finding out about each other and trying to figure out whether you're eventually going to get lucky or not. In the movies you'll just be sitting there side by side, not really being able to hold hands and being very self-conscious. First dates at the movies are embarrassing and unproductive.

However, if she insists on seeing a film try to make sure it's a horror film — then she might cling to you during the grisly bits and that can be an ice-breaker in itself.

So there you are, shaved and scrubbed and she's all stockinged and scented and talking away. It's not easy to ignore the rampant heckler from the dirty side of your mind scrambling your brain when you're trying to make polite conversation:

What's in your head:	*What you say:*	What she says:
Nice tits. I'd love to squeeze them.	What kind of music do you like?	Pretty well anything. I have a fairly catholic taste in music.
Catholic?? This is going to be a problem	Catholic??	Not by religion – I mean I like most stuff – rock, soul, jazz, classical . . . .
Whew. I'd love to kiss those sugary little lips	Oh yeah – me too. who wrote Beethoven's fifth.	Beethoven, silly
I'd like to put my hand down the front of her panties	Heh – just trying to catch you out . . . it's an old joke.	Oh
I wonder if she's wearing tights or those sexy stockings	I like old rock, Buddy Holly and all that stuff	Me too, and I suppose you're a big Elvis fan?
Maybe I'll get to find out later	You bet	You look as if you would be
Imagine undressing her . . .	What's that 'sposed to mean	Oh – I love Elvis, the way he looked an' all . . . no offence.
Wriggling out of those lacy knickers . . .	None taken. What's got 300 legs and no pubic hair?	Dunno
I'd like to pour champagne all over her naked body and lick it all off . . .	The first two rows at a Bros concert.	Hah! Hah! Hah! – most amusing
I wonder if her pubes are blonde as well . . .	Sorry – that was a bit rude. I didn't mean to shock you.	That's okay – I'm very broadminded
Wey Hey!	Yeh, me too.	Hmmm

Don't think we women don't know exactly what you're thinking. It stands out a mile. And the more astute of us know that the brain functions less well when the blood supply has rushed to other parts of your body. We make allowances for that, because it's really quite flattering.

FIRST DATE DOS AND DON'TS

> *Well, if I called the wrong number,*
> *Why did you answer the phone?'*
> *- James Thurber*

On the phone

Be straightforward. Ask her if she'd care to join you for dinner.

Don't beg.

If she says sorry but she's washing her hair suggest another time. If she then says she washes her hair every night, take the hint and forget it.

Don't persist. You'll end up hating yourself.

> *If at first you don't succeed, try again.*
> *Then give up – there's no point making a damn fool of yourself*
> *- W.C. Fields*

What if another man answers the phone? Say, 'This is British Telecom — your phone was reported unobtainable — are you having any problems?'
Don't say 'Who the hell are you?'

FIRST DATE. DO YOU SAY:
a)
What would you like to do?
Go shopping?
Stupid
b)
How about a drink, then dinner and maybe a club later?
Great!
Right
c)
I thought we'd have a few drinks to relax and then back to your place..
Wrong

If you get an answering machine don't leave a message — call back another time.

Don't leave six consecutive messages sounding more desperate each time.

If her flatmate answers, say who you are and ask to speak to the girl you're chasing.
Don't chat up the flatmate and ask if she's sexier than her mate.

If she refuses a date, shrug and put it down to statistics. You win some you lose some.
Don't say, 'Well sod off you silly cow, I never really fancied you anyway'.

THE DATE

Assuming you're going to take her to a cosy restaurant, make sure you book first.
Don't leave it to chance. If you get turned away all you'll get is egg on your face.

Let her know beforehand what you're doing.
Don't surprise her — she could already have eaten and be dressed for a ramble in the woods.

Always insist on paying on a first date.
Don't haggle over splitting the bill, and get all pompous about feminism and equality — you'll just look like a cheapskate.

Compliment her on how wonderful she looks.
Don't tell her that her stockings are wrinkled then find out she's not wearing any.

Keep the party clean.

Don't talk about sex unless she starts it and *don't* be crude even if she is.

On the way home *don't* pounce on her, unless you happen to be getting obviously recognizable signals, in which case still don't pounce. Take it low and slow and if she's keen to see you again that's a big clue that next time anything could happen.

Lunch

One of the best things to do on a first date is to meet for lunch. If one or both of you are working you'll know that sooner or later you'll have to get back, so there's hardly any possibility for seduction. As a result you can both relax and find out if you get on well without worrying about what's going to happen next.

It also gives you a chance to find out what she looks like in daylight. After lunch, if all went well and she's got a sparkle in her eye, you can say, 'Any danger of seeing you one evening?'

Dinner

Dinner can be a strain on a first date. It implies sex and unless both of you are very outgoing it is full of terrible pitfalls. Posh restaurants can make you feel a bit out of your depth. You're more likely to get pissed. And there's the hiatus after dinner of wondering what to do before bedtime. However, there is an outside chance, a very outside chance, that she might turn round to you at her front door and say: 'It's been a wonderful evening — would you like to come in and get laid?'

But Ladbrokes would probably give you odds of 10,000 to one against.

Drinks

If you can't quite remember what she was like from the neck down and want to hedge your bets, you could ask her to meet you for drinks after work. If she's as lovely as you thought you can then ask if she's free for dinner as well. If she's got any class she'll say 'no'.

Breakfast

You got lucky last night.

TEN WAYS TO RUIN A FIRST DATE

- Run out of petrol before you pick her up
- Spill red wine down her front
- Be rude to the waiter
- Get breathalysed
- Have a pee in a shop doorway
- Eat lots of garlic or onions
- Talk while you eat and spray food all over her
- Tell her you hate animals
- Tell her how your last girlfriend who was a blonde, leggy model couldn't stop going down on you

A FIRST DATE NO-NO

9

CONVERSATION

> 'The opposite of talking isn't listening
> The opposite of talking is waiting'
> – Fran Leibowitz

I hate to sound sexist but we girls, by and large, are more articulate than you guys. We are also better dancers but that's another book.

Anyway, sooner or later you'll be sitting opposite a pretty girl, and you will be faced with the need to contribute at least part of the conversation. Nodding isn't enough, in spite of the fact that the most successful Girl Chasers have the knack of getting girls talking about themselves. Once started many girls can go on and on, especially to a mesmerized listener.

HOW TO BLUFF IF YOU'RE NOT A GOOD CONVERSATIONALIST

Think of a few questions to ask her and let her do the talking. Also compliment her on the way she looks.

1) 'Been on holiday?' or 'You look well'
2) 'How do you get on with your mum and dad?' (Good for three hours)

3) 'Nice top — where did you get it?'

Basically this is the Hairdresser Technique again — small talk. It's incredible how many men get by, and are liked by simply everyone (and even on occasion thought of as intelligent) by never talking but just making agreeable sounds: 'Hey . . . OK . . . right . . . yeah man . . . magic!'

Bet you know a few guys like that. It's only a few years later you get found out when your girlfriend or wife suddenly says, 'It's funny but I feel I don't really *know* you.' But by then presumably you've already had your wicked way with her on several occasions — which is what this book's about.

WHAT TO DO WITH SILENCES AND PREGNANT PAUSES

1) Use them to your advantage. A lull in the conversation can be romantic. Glance at her and smile knowingly. Use the opportunity to tickle the back of her hand but only if she's looking at you and not out of the window — otherwise she'll jump out of her skin. You could say something quietly like, 'You have the most beautiful mouth' as if it has just occurred to you. Do *not* say, 'Does curry give you the runs?' or, 'Have you ever found your G-spot?'

2) It isn't a bad idea to have a couple of standard things to say that you can trot out during one of these pauses. The pause itself will act as a prompt and you can find yourself saying, as if to change the subject, 'Princess Anne stays looking young by riding older horses' or possibly, 'God, how I hated India.' Just think of two things, relevant to you, and you can turn a silence into a mini lecture. But don't be boring. And don't say, 'Well . . . shall I get the bill?'

TOPICS TO DISCUSS

Look in the papers to find out what the latest disaster area is, and discuss it. It's bound to be a doomy subject but it should engender a feeling of rapport and empathy between you and the girl you're chasing as well as opening up an opportunity to say something naff like, 'We could always escape into each others' arms.'

The list of disaster topics is endless, but here are some:

- Muggers
- Rapists
- Terrorists
- Car-clampers
- The police
- Bombers
- Plane crashes
- Salmonella
- Lysteria

- The ozone layer
- Rain forests
- South Africa
- Paul Channon
- The channel tunnel
- Rude waiters
- Legionnaires disease
- Junk-mail
- Rees-Mogg

Conspicuous by its absence from this list is AIDS, but for obvious reasons if you're in a seduction mode it's best to avoid this subject if possible until sex looks as if it's definitely on the agenda.

ASTROLOGY

Women are altogether the more spiritual sex and tend to believe in things that are intrinsically nonsensical to the more rational male. The girl you're after is almost bound to believe in one or all of these things:

1) Astrology
2) Reincarnation
3) Flying saucers
4) Ghosts
5) God

The inexperienced Girl Chaser when faced with talking about these topics will rally all his logical arguments, and do his best to de-bunk her beliefs. If he suceeds she'll hate him.

The experienced Girl Chaser is more subtle. He's a pragmatist, and will go along with whatever she says no matter what he really thinks. He knows that his priority is to get into those pants and let her believe what she wants. Terribly cynical, but it works.

So — ask her what birth sign she is and see how she checks out with the following list (if she tells you she's unlisted she's probably a Scorpio) – you never know, there may be something in her after all. Either way, unless it rules your life, it's harmless fun:

Sign	Characteristics	But Can Be
Aries	Energetic, impulsive	Anybodies
Taurus	Sensual, slow to change	Stick in the muds
Gemini	Fun, flirtatious	Schizophrenic or two-faced
Cancer	Loving, emotional	Insecure, mad wierdos that walk sideways into things
Leo	Entertaining, colourful	Show-offs
Virgo	Precise, perfectionists	Frigid/bossy knickers
Libra	Sensitive, balanced, charming	Wishy-washy, indecisive, can't get a good hate out
Scorpio	Passionate/secretive	Intense and selfish
Sagittarius	Adventurous, happy-go-lucky	Born clumsy
Capricorn	Sensible and serious	Boring and dull
Aquarius	Friendly, genius, ahead of their time	Totally on another planet
Pisces	Romantic, mystical	Fey/wet

And because the sun can also affect behaviour patterns, the combination of characteristics becomes even more complex. But suppose as a Girl Chaser you were to make a simple direct statement (not yet if you've only just met her!) here are some possible replies you may get:

You: 'I want to jump on you'
Her:

Aries:	'OK, right now'
Taurus:	'OK, but let's eat first'

Gemini:	'Sure! If I can fit you in somewhere between John and Tony around the 25th of next month'
Cancer:	'Is that a proposal?'
Leo:	'If you're up to it, I'm the best you'll ever get'
Virgo:	'Only if you wear two condoms, and shower before and after'
Libra:	'Nice idea, but on the other hand . . .'
Scorpio:	'See if you can guess my reply'
Sagittarius:	'OK, but somewhere really different'
Capricorn:	'Are you serious? What are your qualifications?'
Aquarius:	'I've always loved violet — it's so surreal'
Pisces:	'I never get jumped on. I only make love'

DOUBLE TALK – HOW TO INTERPRET WHAT SHE MEANS

> *'If you want to know what a woman really means, look at her, do not listen to her'*
> *– Oscar Wilde*

This quote is saying that women universally give more away by what they don't say than by what they do. And often what they do say is not all it seems. Here are some examples:

Says	*Means*
Would you care to come in for coffee?	*I trust you, and maybe we can do it*
I hope we'll be good friends	*If I never see you again it will be too soon*

Your friend Pete looks like a nice guy	*What's his phone number?*
I really like you, but . . .	*Forget it*
I went out with him once	*Once, about twenty times*
He's an asshole	*He never called me again*
I'll call you soon	*Don't call me*
You've got an unusual face	*God, you're ugly*
I'm not ready for a relationship	*Not with you anyway*
You're really sweet	*You're as sexy as a dead dog*
I'm very independent	*I like to go my own way*
What do you do for a living?	*How much do you earn?*
I'm going out with these people tomorrow	*I'm going out with my fiancé, but I don't want you to know I'm involved*
You'd hate Myrtle — she's a real slag	*You'd really fancy her*

Which brings us to the things you should never do in early conversations:

1) *Never* cross examine or grill her
2) *Never* give a list of women you've scored with to give the impression that you're not an inexperienced idiot, because that's exactly the impression you will give
3) *Never* talk about ex-girlfriends. It's irritating, despite the fact that you're no longer with them

4) *Never* brag — it reveals insecurity
5) And above all *never* be disparaging about any woman or women in general

It's a strange thing, but all women have a bond of sisterhood, a kind of female chauvinism that allows us to be as rude and bitchy about other women as we like, while not tolerating men doing the same thing. So *never* refer to girls collectively or individually as the following:

Ground sheets   Floosies
Tarts   Broads

Pussy	Dogs
Bikes	Slags
Beavers	Sluts
	Bits of stuff

And try not to call your date any of these:

Princess	Choochie-face
Babe	Mummy
Kiddo	Busty
Sweetie (particularly irritating)	

There is one, however, that you might get away with: I have a male friend who's bad at remembering names and calls all his girlfriends 'sausage'. For some peculiar reason none of them seem to mind.

10

SEDUCTION

> *'Love is blind, which is why*
> *it has such a keen sense of touch'*
> *– Jayne Mansfield*

OK, it's time for you make your move, and remember nowadays that there's no need for a wolf to dress up in granny's clothes to eat little girls. Not unless you're really weird, anyway.

Firstly the timing and the atmosphere must be right. Soft lights, music all that kind of stuff. It also helps to know if she's in the mood, and steam coming out of her ears is a big clue.

It's a fact of life that while men get to do the asking, women call the shots. Outside of rape, we control when and where seduction can happen. We do it when we're good and ready or not at all. It's up to you to make us good and ready though, and quite often it doesn't take a lot. So before you go in for the kill make sure she isn't already dead. We modern women aren't as prim as our grannies used to be. We still have our virtue, but we hardly ever use it any more.

The more romantic the atmosphere the better your chances:

Romantic	*Unromantic*
MUSIC	
The best of Julie London	Heavy metal
Old-fashioned stuff in general	Heavy classics
LIGHTING	
Soft, diffused, preferably log fire.	Strip lights
Candlelight — it's more flattering	Spot lights that dazzle
SMELLS	
Good aftershave	Stale cigarettes
Fresh coffee	Boozy breath
Fresh flowers, and if you're lucky,	Stale sweat
jasmin on a hot summer's night	
PLACES	
Her place	Your place
Venice	Brussels
Paris	Birmingham
Barcelona	Warsaw
Key West	Philadelphia
FOOD	
Oysters	Eels
Champagne	Lager
Asparagus	Mushy peas
Expensive chocolates	Kitkat bar

TEST:
Which of these girls is in the mood?

a)

b)

Who said (b)? Stick to football.

SOME WAYS OF GETTING IT RIGHT AND WRONG

Right

A four-poster bed with twenty lit candles to *Carmina Burana* — Venice with a bottle of Dom Perignon champagne

Wrong

Over the ironing board to 'Pomp and Circumstance' by Elgar, in Milton Keynes with a few cans of Newcastle Brown

Right

A balcony in Manhattan at dusk, to 'Shades of Spain' by Miles Davies with Melon Margueritas

Wrong

On top of the Managing Director's desk while he's out at lunch to 'If I Ruled the World' by Harry Secombe

Right

Long grass in Richmond Park on a sunny afternoon. No music — so you can hear if anyone's coming

TRAVELLING ABROAD BY PLANE

If you've managed to persuade her to spend a week with you in some exotic part of the world the main thing is to make it as romantic as possible.

Travelling together is romantically counter-productive as can be seen from the following typical sequence:

    1) Arrive at airport. Check-in. Who has the tickets? Who has the passports? A stressful time – *2 hours*

2) A long tiring plane journey – *9 hours*
3) Arrive late (you always do)
4) Baggage claim. Immigration, customs — with heavy cases – *At least 1 hour*
5) Car rental, long queues with heavy bags – *1 hour minimum*
6) By now you're very tired and irritable
7) Drive to hotel. Where is it? – *1 hour*
8) Check in at hotel. Form filling – *Embarrassment*
9) Find room. No change to tip porter – *Embarrassment*
10) Flop on bed exhausted, smelly, bad tempered and thoroughly pissed off with each other. No way to start a holiday – *No bonk*

But there is a better way to do it. You can't avoid the hassles of travel but you can minimize them. Here's what you do:

1) You travel out a day earlier than her. Men usually have less luggage so you won't have to hump hers
2) The plane journey is easier because you can sleep without having her leaning on you
3) You get the hire car and check in at the hotel
4) She arrives on the next day. By now you've got everything organized and are feeling relaxed
5) You have a romantic meeting at the airport. Although she's quite tired you take her bags and whisk her away in the waiting car to the hotel and straight to the room. No fuss, no hanging about
6) You have a drink in the bar while she has a bath and recuperates
7) Dinner and bonk, or bonk and dinner, or both, or either

That's how the experienced Girl Chaser does it. And there are two other advantages, less romantic.

1) If you want to impress her you can buy her a First, or Club-class ticket without having to fork out for one for yourself (or vice versa)
2) You stand less chance of being seen together by your wife/girlfriend/children/paparazzi

KISSING

> 'His kissing left nothing to be desired –
> except the rest of him'
> – A friend of mine – about a friend of hers

Years ago I laughed out loud at a John Glasham cartoon showing two Hoo-rays talking in their club:

A: 'How did you get on with Lady Sarah last night?'
B: 'Oh, quite well, but she made me kiss her first'

Funny though it is, I'm sad to say that this sums up the attitude of many men. They use kissing as a means to an end, artillery to storm a fortress, without actually enjoying it much.

Women love men who enjoy kissing. It turns us on more than anything else for one very good reason: Kissing is the most intimate thing two people can do together.

Think about it.

And ask any hooker. Girls on the game will do anything for money. Sex in any position — any weird perversion — orgies, you name it. But no amount of money will get them to kiss you passionately if they don't feel anything for you. And why? It's too intimate.

Kissing someone she can't stand makes a girl feel sick. But kissing someone she fancies makes her melt.

So it's worth remembering that if a girl can't get enough of your kisses you're home and dry, except dry is probably the wrong word.

Kissing checklist

1) Have clean teeth
2) Be tender to start with and get progressively more passionate
3) Vary the intensity of your kisses in response to her
4) Tease her a bit with your tongue
5) Touch her face and the back of her neck gently
6) Smile if you catch her looking at you
7) Nibble her neck
8) Leave her wanting more

Don't

1) Ram your tongue straight down her throat
2) Give gooey, wet, open-mouthed kisses
3) Kiss with your mouth shut
4) Get so carried away she can't kiss you back
5) Pin her down so she can hardly breathe
6) Bite her ear
7) Fart
8) Outstay your welcome
9) Assume she's going to let you go any further

KISSING Rule 53: Wait for her to put down the frying pan.

THE NEXT PHASE

> *'A frosty young lady from Ealing*
> *Professed to lack sexual feeling*
> *But a cynic called Boris,*
> *Just touched her clitoris*
> *And she had to be scraped from the ceiling'*

Groping, foreplay, slap'n'tickle, call it what you will, this is the bit where the hands start wandering and if she's anything other than a brazen hussy she'll push them away as a token gesture. If, however she pushes them away more than ten times, be nice and pack it in.

'He who gropes and runs away, lives to grope another day'

Besides, she may have a period, but can't use that as an excuse because it would amount to an open admission that next time you're going to get lucky.

SOME USEFUL TIPS FOR FOREPLAY

1) Take your time. This means spend time fondling her and getting her aroused. It doesn't mean reading the paper, having a long bath and then jumping on her

2) Vary your touch. This means using your hands and your mouth intelligently all over her body. It does not mean trying out different women

3) Caress her whole body top to bottom. This means that the whole of a woman's body becomes aroused, not just the

obvious sexy bits. It doesn't mean give her a big bear hug, then quick rumpy pumpy

I forgot to mention that before all this, it's a good idea to remove her clothing (and yours, naturally). This is an art in itself. Undressing a girl is part of the fun like unwrapping a present. Especially if the wrapping is sexy and pretty, in which case you may like to leave some of it on.

> *Girl: (looking at tarty high-heeled strappy sandals.)*
> *'How could I possibly walk in those?'*
> *Wicked Willie: 'You don't. You take them off*
> *the moment you get out of bed'*

WAYS A MAN SHOULD UNDRESS

> *'The Dean undressed with heaving breast*
> *The bishop's wife to lie on*
> *He thought it lewd*
> *To do it nude*
> *So kept his old school tie on'*

1) Let her do it for you
2) Item for item with her — like strip poker
3) Leave everything on until she's completely nude. This in itself can be quite a turn-on for both of you
4) When you do get undressed chuck everything on the floor. *Do not* hang things up or fold them carefully.
5) Undress in the right order. First shoes and socks. *Never ever* leave your socks till last. (A naked man wearing socks looks like someone from a Danish porno magazine and is a total and utter turn-off). Then shirt, and last trousers and briefs or whatever it is you wear

Wrong

UNDRESSING

← Right

WAYS TO UNDRESS A GIRL

1) Let her do it by herself like a striptease
2) Always undress her standing up anyway. Wriggling out of woollies and dresses while lying on a bed is not very becoming

3) By all means take her to bed in her bra and panties and stockings. Even in her stilettos, although it's not a bad idea to remove these before she starts kicking holes in the duvet

FINDING THE G-SPOT

> 'To bed, to sleep perchance to dream
> of better ways to come. Aye, but where do you rub?'
> – Shakespearish

You may or may not find the apocryphal G-spot. But you certainly won't find it unless you go through the rest of the alphabet first. See diagram.

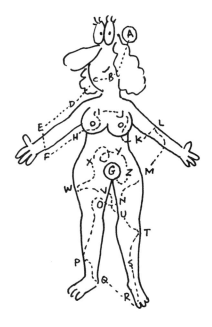

DOING IT

> *'It's not the length of the wand that matters, but the magic in it'*

That's all you need to know. This book is not about fucking. It is about Girl Chasing and if you've got this far you have clearly caught one. So you're on your own from here, buddy — there's nothing worse than love-making instruction books. When you do it, you do it your way.

> *'I Did It My Way'*
> *– Frank Sinatra*

> *'Is sex dirty?*
> *Only if you do it right'*
> *– Woody Allen*

11

SOME THINGS IT MAY HELP YOU TO KNOW

BIG 'O'

Jane: 'Why is it 100 per cent of men have
orgasms when they make love and only 4
per cent of women do?'
John: 'Who cares?'

Sums it up. But you *should* care, and that takes patience. In 1977 B. J. Friedman wrote, 'In the case of some women, orgasms take quite a bit of time. Before signing on with such a partner make sure you are willing to lay aside, say, the month of June, with sandwiches having to be brought in.'
Did you know:

1) Girls can have orgasms 100 per cent of the time, but only when they're on their own
2) Girls often fake orgasms
3) Every girl has her own special way of having an orgasm. The secret is to get her to tell you what it is
4) On average, a woman's sexual organ is twenty inches in circumference. I am, of course, referring to her brain
5) Girls can find sex fulfilling even if they don't have an orgasm, but don't push your luck

A TOTAL AND UTTER PRAT

> '*Mummy, mummy, what's an orgasm?*'
> '*Shut up and ask your father when he gets home*'

CONTRACEPTION AND THE FEMALE CYCLE

> '*Contraception should be used
> on every conceivable occasion.*'
> – *Spike Milligan*

Absolutely right, but don't assume that she's taken care of it. Here's a summary of the common methods.

Type and Effectiveness	Advantage	Disadvantage
Condoms (95% effective)	No side effects and can act as a shield against sexually transmitted diseases	Can feel like picking your nose with a glove on
The cap and spermicides (Prevents sperm entering womb, 85–97% effective)	No side effects, although spermicides can irritate some girls	It can interfere with spontaneous lovemaking as it can turn into a frisbee and thwang about the bathroom especially if trying to insert it in a hurry
The Coil (It prevents fertilized egg from implanting in the uterus wall), 96–98% effective)	Nothing to do or think about so sex can be spontaneous	It can feel like a staple-gun for men in certain positions. Heavier periods and risk of pelvic infection and ectopic pregnancy
The Honey Cap (same as other cap only no spermicide as there's a theory that honey is a natural spermicide)	No fuss. You can leave it in as long as you want	One major side-effect for many women is pregnancy. Basically it doesn't work
The Pill (taken daily for certain days prevents the release of eggs, 98% effective)	Easy to use. No interference with sex	Headaches, high blood pressure, weight gain, varicose veins, mood swings
Mini Pill (98% effective)	Same as above	It must be taken at exactly the same time every day

Oral contraception (talking your way out of it)	Cheap	Unreliable
Foams/Jellies (Kills or immobilizes sperm, 20% pregnancy rate)	Easy to obtain	Gooey and yukky. Has to be continually reapplied. Tastes disgusting.
Rhythm Method (sex only in the infertile time, i.e. before and after safe ovulation time. The time of ovulation is discovered by keeping records of period dates and temperature changes)	No pills or devices	It's not reliable if periods aren't reliable. Limits sex. Have to keep scrupulous records.
Female Condom	No physical side effects	Great – if used as a sail on a windsurf.
Asprin (Held firmly between the knees)	Readily available	You may lose it
Sterilization (Man: Prevents sperm being released into seminal fluid) (Woman: Blocks the passage of the egg from the ovaries to the uterus. Virtually 100% effective)	No need to think about contraception	It's pretty well final

Position of the Moon (When the new moon corresponds to the new moon in your natal chart, you can be fertile regardless of the cycle)	You're one up on the rhythm method	You have to do a lot of sky-watching

'A' FEMALE CYCLE.
'THE' FEMALE CYCLE
IS SOMETHING ELSE

How the Female Cycle Works

1) The whole cycle can take between twenty-eight to thirty-four days to complete depending on the girl

2) A girl ovulates on the fourteenth day of a cycle

3) If fertilization doesn't take place, the womb will shed its lining (known as a period) and the process begins again

4) A lot of girls get premenstrual tension a week before a period and this can include: depression, irritation, bloatedness, water retention, headaches, over-emotionalism

5) Sperm lives from two to five days and an egg lives for two to three days, therefore in a cycle, days nine to eighteen are potential days for conception

Tips for dealing with pre-menstrual tension

1) Keep dates on a calendar and go on a business trip that week
2) Find out how it affects her so you're prepared for it
3) Don't say 'Is it your period?' or if you do, act tactfully not blamefully
4) Don't treat her like a leper and make barfing faces
5) Don't ignore her and pretend all is normal. She is affected
6) Be prepared for anything
7) Be considerate
8) Don't take any rows in this time too seriously
9) Just be aware it is a reality, don't be threatened by it and don't take it personally

12

BUT WILL IT LAST?

'Do you feel the excitement has gone out of our relationship?'
'Let's discuss it during the next commercial break'
                                                    – Milton Berle

You've chased her, you've caught her, and much to your surprise you want to keep her. How do you stop the magic fading?

Don't allow yourself to be dominated. Women will always try to dominate men, not that we really want to, but subconsciously we like to put you to the test, to see what you're made of. You must resist — we look up to men who stand up to us.

And don't allow yourself to get lazy. We expect you to carry on the way you started out otherwise you can expect any or all of the following manifestations of the 'Not Tonight' syndrome:

    1) 'I've got a headache'
    2) 'My period has lasted three weeks'
    3) 'I'm totally bushwacked'
    4) 'Not *here* darling' (wherever you are)
    5) 'Someone might hear us'
    6) Pretends to be asleep
    7) Starts an argument

8) 'Rather watch TV'
9) 'Got a strange discharge'
10) 'I've got to get up'

The reason behind this reluctance is probably that you:

1) Came home drunk and slept downstairs with the dog
2) Forgot to come home at all
3) Watch TV for hours without talking
4) Never compliment her cooking
5) Come too soon and fall asleep
6) Work late every night
7) Get brewer's droop
8) Fart in bed
9) Snore all night
10) Got spots on it (measles??)

Moody silences are usually a sign that things are not as they should be. But don't say, 'What's up with you?', because she'll only say, 'Nothing'. Ignore it, and pretty soon it will come to the surface and you can decide whether it's worth carrying on or not.

Meanwhile try and avoid the following lines, unless you want her to throw the toaster at you:

a) 'Is it your period that's making you act so odd?'
b) 'My work is none of your business — you wouldn't understand it anyway'
c) 'You're just imagining it'
d) 'You're getting just like your mother'
e) 'Are you seriously going out looking like that?'
f) 'Honestly, it was only sex. She means nothing to me.'
g) 'I don't want to discuss it . . .'

THE BEGINNING OF THE END

So what can you do?

Good question. You probably started off by sweeping her off her feet — sending her flowers and cards, buying her little presents, opening the car door for her. Trouble is, when you start like that and end up getting what you want, you start doing it less, and eventually not at all. And then all those things become very conspicuous by their absence.

So if you started out nice stay nice. I know it takes effort but only you can tell whether the effort is worth it.

And if it isn't try these :

1) Suggest a 'trial separation'
2) Say you need space to 'find yourself'
3) Move abroad
4) Do a vanishing act
5) Introduce your wife
6) Introduce your kids
7) Always be late
8) Behave in a gross and drunken manner all the time
9) Introduce her to a richer, better looking friend
10) Have a blatant affair
11) Tell her you're bisexual
12) Give her crabs
13) Have a sex change
14) 'Get' religion
15) Tell her you're an alien and have to get back to Betelgeuse
16) Push her under a bus
17) Bonk her best friend
18) Join the Foreign Legion
19) Die

That should do it. Now back to square one.